THE NATURE KIDS GUIDE TO

RACCOONS

DAVID ANDERSON

LP Media Inc. Publishing
Text copyright © 2026 by LP Media Inc.
All rights reserved.

For information address LP Media Inc. Publishing,
30012 Variolite St NW, Princeton MN 55371
www.lpmedia.org

Publication Data

Raccoons
The Nature Kid's Guide to Raccoons — First edition.

Summary: "Learn all about Raccoons, the Nature Kid Way"
— Provided by publisher.

ISBN: 979-8-89818-119-2

[1. Raccoons – Non-Fiction] I. Title.

Title: The Nature Kid's Guide to Raccoons

CONTENTS

HOME SWEET HOME

Rustle! A raccoon peeks out from a hollow tree. Its masked face looks out.

Raccoons love places with trees and water. They need forests with streams or ponds nearby. Swamps make perfect homes too.

These clever animals like mild weather best. But they can handle cold winters and hot summers. They just need a cozy den to rest in.

Raccoons find shelter in tree holes and rock cracks. They also use old burrows dug by other animals. In towns, they sleep in attics and sheds. They pick spots that feel safe and dry.

ROAMING RANGE

Snap! A raccoon walks through tall grass, exploring new land.

Raccoons live all over North and Central America. They roam from Canada to Panama.

The common raccoon lives in the United States and Mexico. The crab-eating raccoon lives in Central America.

Raccoons live on islands too. They live in the Florida Keys. They also live in parts of the Caribbean.

The crab-eating raccoon lives in South America and loves to catch crabs, lobsters, and crayfish from rivers. It uses its super-sensitive hands to find food underwater!

7

SIZE CHECK

Thump! A raccoon sits on a log. It looks round and fluffy.

Raccoons are medium-sized mammals. They are bigger than house cats but smaller than dogs. Most raccoons weigh between 10 and 30 pounds.

Male raccoons are usually larger than females. In fall, some males weigh even more. They gain extra weight before winter comes.

A raccoon's body is about two feet long. Its bushy tail adds another ten inches.

The heaviest wild raccoon on record weighed over 60 pounds. That is bigger than most dogs!

MASKED MARVELS
DID YOU KNOW?
A raccoon's back feet can rotate 180 degrees. This helps them climb down trees headfirst.

Click! A raccoon taps its paws on a branch. Its sharp claws grip tight.

Raccoons have special body features. Their gray and brown fur keeps them warm. Black rings circle their fluffy tails. The stripes confuse predators and help raccoons blend in with tree branches.

The dark mask across a raccoon's face is easy to spot. This black fur wraps around both eyes. White fur frames the mask above and below.

Raccoons have five fingers on each paw. Their front paws work almost like hands. Sharp claws help them climb and dig. Their strong back legs also help them run and jump.

SUPER SENSES

Sniff! A raccoon lifts its nose. It sniffs the night air.

Raccoons have amazing senses. Their hearing is very sharp, they can hear mice moving through leaves or insects buzzing in trees.

A raccoon's sense of touch is special. Their front paws feel things underwater. This helps them find food without seeing it.

A special layer in their eyes reflects light, helping them hunt at night.

A raccoons front paws have four times more touch sensors than it's back paws.

STAY SAFE

Growl! A raccoon puffs up its fur. It looks bigger now.

Raccoons have several ways to protect themselves. They can bite and scratch with sharp teeth and claws. They have thick fur to protect their skin.

When scared, raccoons make loud sounds. They hiss, growl, and screech at enemies. This can scare predators away.

Raccoons also puff up their fur. This makes them look even larger than they are. Sometimes looking big is enough to stay safe.

Raccoons can run up to 15 miles per hour. That's as fast as most adult humans!

DID YOU KNOW?

TRASH TREATS

Crunch! A raccoon eats an apple core it found in a trash can.

Raccoons eat many different foods. They are **omnivores**, which means they eat both plants and animals.

In the wild, raccoons eat berries, nuts, and insects. They also catch frogs, fish, and crayfish. They even snack on bird eggs when they find them.

Near people, raccoons find easy meals. They tip over trash cans and dig through garbage. Pet food left outside becomes raccoon food.

Raccoons often dunk food in water to feel it better.

GRABBY HANDS

Raccoons have five fingers on each paw, just like humans have five fingers.

Splash! A raccoon dips its paws into a cool stream. It searches for food.

Raccoons use their front paws like hands. Their long, flexible fingers grab, hold, and turn objects easily.

When hunting in water, raccoons feel around with their paws. They reach under rocks and logs to grab crayfish, clams, and small fish. Their sensitive paws find prey they cannot see.

On land, raccoons use their paws to open things. They can turn doorknobs and lift latches. They also peel back bark to find insects hiding underneath. Their clever paws help them find food almost anywhere.

WATCH OUT

Snarl! A coyote spots a raccoon near a fence. The raccoon freezes.

Raccoons have many predators. Coyotes and Bobcats hunt them. Bobcats hunt them. Mountain lions hunt them too.

Great horned owls hunt for young raccoons at night.

In some areas, alligators catch raccoons near water. Foxes and large hawks even hunt small raccoons.

But the biggest threats to raccons are cars. Many are hit trying to cross the road at night.

Mother raccoons fiercely attack predators to protect their babies.

RUN AND HIDE

Whoosh! A raccoon spots a predator and darts up a tree trunk fast.

Raccoons have many ways to escape danger. Running away is often the first choice.

But climbing is their best escape trick. Raccoons scramble up trees in seconds. They hide in high branches until danger passes.

When near water, raccoons can swim to safety. They paddle across ponds and streams. Raccoons can even drown a predator that follows them into the water.

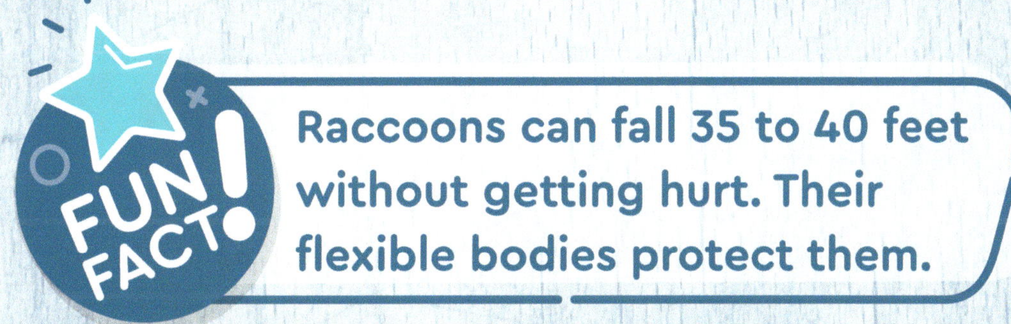

CLIMB HIGH

Jump! A raccoon climbs a wooden fence, heading up toward the roof.

Raccoons are great climbers. They climb trees. They climb fences. They climb buildings too. Their strong back legs push them up.

Raccoons can turn their back feet all the way around. Their feet can point backwards. This helps them go down trees headfirst.

They climb to find food. They climb to find shelter. Raccoons also climb to get away from predators.

Raccoons have climbed skyscrapers in cities, sometimes reaching over 20 stories high.

NIGHT SHIFT

Hoot! An owl calls in the dark. Nearby, a raccoon wakes up.

Raccoons are **nocturnal**. This means they are active at night. They sleep during the day in dens or hollow trees.

At dusk, raccoons wake up and start moving. They spend the night searching for food. Their excellent night vision helps them see well in the dark.

Raccoons return to their dens before sunrise. They sleep through the bright daylight hours.

Raccoons are most active right after sunset and may travel several miles in one night searching for food.

GANG GOALS

Chirp! Young raccoons play together near a log.

Raccoons often live alone as adults. But young raccoons grow up together. Female raccoons may even share dens with other females.

Mothers and their young stay together for many months. Young raccoons learn and play as a group.

Male raccoons sometimes travel together too. These small bands share food sources in their area.

A group of raccoons is called a gaze or a nursery. Babies stay with mom for one year.

FINDING FRIENDS

Squeak! A raccoon calls out in the spring night air.

Raccoons mate once a year. This happens in late winter or early spring, usually between January and March.

Male raccoons travel far. They may visit many different females' territories, sometimes walking several miles in one night!

After mating, the males leave. The females raise babies alone. Baby raccoons are born about 63 days later.

Female raccoons sometimes adopt orphaned baby raccoons and raise them alongside their own kits.

CUTE KITS

DID YOU KNOW?
Raccoon kits are born with faint mask markings. The dark fur around their eyes gets darker as they grow.

Pounce! A tiny raccoon kit tumbles in the leaves. Its mother watches nearby.

Baby raccoons are called **kits**. They are born in spring, and a mother usually has three to five kits at once.

Newborn kits are very small. They weigh only about three ounces. Their eyes stay closed for the first three weeks.

Kits grow quickly. By two months old, they start exploring outside the den. They follow their mother everywhere.

Young raccoons stay with their mother through their first winter. They learn important skills before living on their own.

MAMA KNOWS

DID YOU KNOW?

Mother raccoons purr and chirp to their kits. They growl at danger.

Grunt! A mother raccoon carries her kit by the scruff.

Mother raccoons do all the parenting work. They raise their kits without help from male raccoons.

These busy mothers keep their babies safe in dens. They move their kits to new dens if danger comes near. A careful mother may have several backup dens ready.

Mother raccoons also teach their young how to find food. They show kits how to climb and forage. Kits watch and copy what their mother does.

By fall, young raccoons know many survival skills. They are ready to move out and live on their own.

RACCOON RESILIENCE

Rustle! A raccoon digs through leaves. It finds food.

Raccoons are tough animals. They can adapt to live almost anywhere.

If one food source is scarce, they find another. If forests are cut down, they find ways to live near cities.

Raccoons are smart problem solvers. They can open jars and doors. Their intelligence has helped them survive and **flourish** over time.

Raccoons can survive cold winters by sleeping in dens. They do not truly hibernate but rest for weeks at a time.

RACCOON WATCH

Rustle! A raccoon pokes its head out at dusk.

You can watch raccoons in many places. They almost certainly live nearby, even if you haven't seen them. Look for them near water. Look for them near trees.

Raccoons come out at night. Dusk is the best time to see them. Stay quiet. Stay still. Bring a flashlight. Put a red cover on it.

Watch from far away. Raccoons are wild animals. Never feed them. Do not get too close.

Raccoons have excellent night vision. Their eyes reflect light, making them glow in the dark.

GLOSSARY

hibernate
To sleep through the whole winter to save energy

flourish
To survive and grow in numbers.

kits
Baby raccoons.

nocturnal
Active at night and sleeping during the day.

omnivores
Animals that eat both plants and other animals.